IMAGES
of America

GREETINGS FROM BERTRAND ISLAND AMUSEMENT PARK

For more than 70 years, New Jersey's largest lake was the spot for summertime fun at Bertrand Island Amusement Park, seen here in 1975.

IMAGES
of America

GREETINGS FROM BERTRAND ISLAND AMUSEMENT PARK

Martin and Laura Kane

ARCADIA

First printed in 2000.

Published by Arcadia Publishing,
an imprint of Tempus Publishing, Inc.
2 Cumberland Street
Charleston, SC 29401

Printed in Great Britain.

Library of Congress Catalog Card Number: 00-104059

For all general information contact Arcadia Publishing at:
Telephone 843-853-2070
Fax 843-853-0044
E-Mail sales@arcadiapublishing.com

For customer service and orders:
Toll-Free 1-888-313-2665

Visit us on the internet at http://www.arcadiapublishing.com

This is a souvenir button for Bertrand Island Park on Lake Hopatcong.

CONTENTS

ACKNOWLEDGMENTS

Begun as an outgrowth of a video project, this book became a labor of love. We hope it will bring back fond memories to those who enjoyed the park, and document the fun that was Bertrand Island Park for those who did not have the opportunity to visit.

The book would not have been possible without the wonderful resources of the Lake Hopatcong Historical Museum. Though there is not enough space here to list all the names, we wish to express our gratitude to the hundreds of people who have donated photographs or allowed photographs to be copied by the museum. We sincerely appreciate your generosity in entrusting us with your souvenirs, artifacts, and memories of the park. You have ensured that the history of Bertrand Island Park is documented and preserved. A brass ring to each of you!

Special thanks must go to Ray D'Agostino and the Cuda family for having preserved such large collections of memorabilia pertaining to Bertrand Island and for graciously sharing them with the museum. In addition, many thanks to Ray for all the advice and firsthand knowledge he brought to this project. We are also greatly indebted to Fred Shay for having the foresight to salvage Bertrand Island scrapbooks from likely destruction and the kindness to donate them to the Lake Hopatcong Historical Museum. Also, sincere thanks to Rick Bucci, Al Cuda, the late Ed Cuda, Mike Fasino, Donald McElroy, and Anne Woda for sharing their memories and reminiscences of the park. We must also thank the good people at the National Amusement Park Historical Association, whose archives were most helpful in our research.

And finally, a big hug to our daughter Natalie for her genuine enthusiasm for the project. We wish she could have visited Bertrand Island. Oh yes, thanks to Lucky Dog for putting up with the late nights this book required.

We hope that *Greetings from Bertrand Island Amusement Park* will bring the same enjoyment to the readers as its creation has brought the writers.

INTRODUCTION

Growing up, many of us thought it would be around forever. A trip there marked the start of summer. The 100 or so days it was open each year were special at Lake Hopatcong. For a few nickels, we could have one heck of a good time. Bertrand Island was our local amusement park. It was not as well known as Palisades Park, and it was not as large and spectacular as the Disney or Six Flags giants were. But the park had a comfortable feeling. We knew just where everything was, and we knew most of the concessionaires by name. It may have had just 20 rides, but we never tired of going.

Bertrand Island Park marked the last vestiges of an earlier era—a time when Lake Hopatcong was a bustling resort that supported hotels, pavilions, and endless activities. The park ultimately fell victim to this New Jersey area's coming of age as a year-round community. While Bertrand Island was able to survive two world wars and the Great Depression, it could not survive a booming local economy.

Gone for almost 20 years now, it is still fondly remembered. The mention of its name brings happy memories to thousands. For as much as the park was built of wood and steel and nails, it was made of music and laughter and fun.

With heartfelt thanks to all those who made the existence and operation of the park possible, we bring you *Greetings from Bertrand Island Amusement Park.*

One
THE MOUNTAIN
LAKE PARADISE

Bertrand Island is located on the eastern shore of Lake Hopatcong in the Borough of Mount Arlington. Though it appears to be a sleepy place in this 1910 photograph taken from the lake's west shore, events occurring on the other side of the island soon were to make the name Bertrand Island synonymous with fun.

LAKE HOPATCONG
FROM COL. GREENS

Bertrand Island is a peninsula today, but it was once an island separated from the mainland by a narrow channel. In the early 1860s, Charles Bertrand purchased significant land at Lake Hopatcong, which was then a remote, sparsely populated area of New Jersey. Bertrand built a grand home for his family on the island that later bore his name. Bertrand died in 1870, and the house burned in the ensuing years. This *c.* 1910 photograph shows the small bridge that linked the island to the mainland.

Bertrand Island was subsequently sold to a group of men who built a clubhouse on the old foundation of the Bertrand home. Known as the Bertrand Island Club, it was typical of the men's clubs common at the time—a place to hunt and fish, play cards, and drink a little whiskey. During the summer, club members took turns bringing their families to the lake. In the 1890s, the Bertrand Island Club was destroyed by fire. Members are seen in front of the club in this early photograph.

While Bertrand Island was originally separated from the mainland by a larger body of water, over the years the area was filled so that only a small bridge was needed.

The wooden bridge, seen here in 1907, allowed horses and wagons, as well as early automobiles, to reach Bertrand Island from Mount Arlington. The bridge remained in place until the 1920s, when the land separating the mainland and island was filled in and amusements were built on this area.

Following the destruction of the Bertrand Island Club in the 1890s, there was little use made of Bertrand Island until 1905, when the island was purchased by a group of businessmen with ambitious development plans.

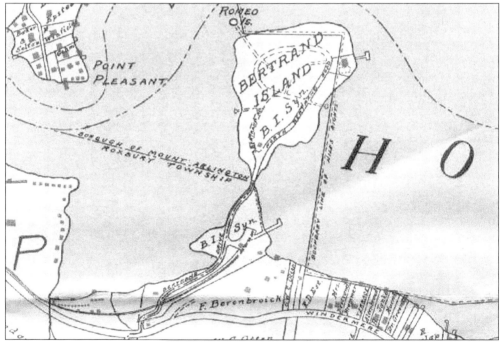

The island was divided into 257 lots, each about 50 by 110 feet. At the center of the island, about 4 acres were reserved for a hotel. The group proposed, among other plans, moving one of the casinos used at the St. Louis Exposition of 1904 to the island. This 1912 map shows the land owned by the Bertrand Island syndicate.

The business syndicate's plans also included direct train service to Bertrand Island and steamer service to all parts of the lake. While these grandiose ideas never materialized, the group was responsible for creating a beach on its proposed development in 1905, as seen in this photograph taken shortly after construction.

The beach at Bertrand Island quickly became a popular spot for swimming at the lake. As shown in this 1907 postcard, it began to be called "Little Coney" after New York's famous Coney Island.

Though a hotel was operating on its shore as early as 1859, Lake Hopatcong was largely unknown until train service began in 1882, sparking a tremendous boom for this quiet region of northwestern New Jersey. Hotels, stores, and amusements quickly arose to serve the new tourist trade. By 1900, Lake Hopatcong was home to over 40 hotels and rooming houses.

The Bertrand Island beach was a perfect destination for the thousands of vacationers arriving at Lake Hopatcong. Businesses developed to cater to the beachcombers, and soon the beach at Bertrand Island became so popular that it caught the attention of the Morris County Traction Company.

Two
"Clang Clang Clang" Went the Trolley

Trolley construction swept across America in the latter part of the 19th century. In a time just before the automobile and bus became commonplace, the trolley provided an inexpensive form of transportation for relatively short distances. The Morris County Traction Company introduced trolleys to northwestern New Jersey. At its peak, the Morris County Traction Company's service stretched from Newark and Elizabeth to Lake Hopatcong. Chartered in 1899, its line eventually reached Bertrand Island. Trolley service proved to be a main factor in Bertrand Island's development, as witnessed by this happy party arriving at the island in the early 1920s.

Blackwell Street, Dover, N. J.

Dover was the first town to receive trolley service from the Morris County Traction Company. As seen in this *c.* 1909 photograph, the trolley tracks ran on Blackwell Street, the town's main commercial artery. Service began between Dover and Wharton in 1904 and expanded to Rockaway later that year.

CHURCH AND LAKE
LEDGEWOOD, N.J.

The trolley headed west from Dover through Wharton, Mine Hill, Kenvil, Succasunna, and Ledgewood. This *c.* 1910 photograph shows the trolley proceeding along Main Street in Ledgewood.

The Morris County Traction Company reached Landing in 1908. This *c*. 1912 photograph shows the trolley passing the recently completed Lackawanna Railroad station before crossing over the railroad tracks and ending its service by the steamboat dock at Landing.

Like trolley lines across America, the Morris County Traction Company was looking for ways to increase use on weekends. Nationwide, many amusement parks and recreational facilities were established at the end of trolley lines for just this reason. Following some difficulties in obtaining the right to use existing railroad tracks, the Morris County Traction Company was able to expand its service from Landing to the popular beach at Bertrand Island. This *c*. 1908 photograph shows the trolley in Landing by the Lackawanna Railroad bridge that survives today.

On Decoration Day (now Memorial Day) 1910, trolley service to Bertrand Island began, making the beach accessible to large numbers of people living in northern New Jersey. This *c.* 1910 photograph shows the trolley stop at Landing across from the steamboat dock. From here the trolley turned right, on its way to Bertrand Island. The trip from Morristown to Bertrand Island took about two hours and cost 35¢.

As travelers began arriving by trolley, food stands and amusements were built just off the beach. As seen in this 1910 photograph, Schaefer's Hotel, of Mount Arlington, established a restaurant at the end of the trolley line. The trolley remained a popular link to Bertrand Island for some 15 years, although during World War I, service was terminated at Landing so that the trolley would not interfere with trains bound for Atlas Powder Company, an explosives manufacturer then located along the lake's east shore.

ERTRAND ISLAND PARK

DANCING EVERY EVENING AND SATURDAY AFTERNOON.

Cool open air pavilion, fifty feet above the water, facing lake on three sides.

GOOD ORCHESTRA   EXCELLENT FLOORS
CARROUSEL   REFRESHMENTS

ed by Trolley and Boat   Free Dockage for Parties for the Park at Bertrand Island Termin

As witnessed by this 1913 advertisement, a large open-air dance pavilion, carousel, and other activities soon followed the introduction of trolley service. By 1917, the beach at Bertrand Island included a shooting range, water chute, and diving float.

Boats were an integral part of Bertrand Island from the outset. A large dock, seen in this 1910 photograph, was built near the beach just after its opening so that the lake's steamboats could drop off vacationers wishing to visit. The Morris County Traction Company offered moonlight excursions to Lake Hopatcong. One dollar would purchase a round-trip ticket from Morristown, which included a boat ride on the lake.

The Bertrand Island Transportation Company, a descendant of the competing steamboat companies from the lake's early years, had its headquarters at Bertrand Island and provided service around the lake. This 1910 photograph and the photograph below show the Bertrand Island Transportation Company's fleet.

When the Bertrand Island Transportation Company fleet was destroyed by a March 1923 fire at Bertrand Island, it was the last large fleet at Lake Hopatcong. Automobiles were becoming an increasingly popular alternate means of transportation. As Americans fell in love with automobiles, trolley service also suffered. The Morris County Traction Company ended service in 1926 and was replaced by buses. By then, Bertrand Island Park was solidly established.

Three

A DREAM BECOMES REALITY

Bertrand Island Park evolved during the golden age of amusement parks. Following the tremendous success of the midway at the 1893 Chicago World's Fair and the *c.* 1900 parks at Coney Island, New York, amusement parks rapidly spread throughout the United States. By 1919, more than 1,500 were in operation nationwide. In this 1922 photograph, a family arrives for a day of fun at just such a place—Bertrand Island Park.

The guiding force behind Bertrand Island Park's emergence as an amusement park was Louis Kraus, a schoolteacher from Newark. He and his wife, Elsie Kraus, started a new business in the summer of 1908 called Camp Village in the Prospect Point section of Lake Hopatcong.

At this time, the lake was not yet widely developed, and camping appealed to many visitors. Camp Village catered to families, providing a less expensive alternative to hotels and, as Kraus pointed out in his literature, "none of the midnight revelry of the hotel parlor to disturb your rest."

For about $6 per week, a family could rent one of the camp's tents, complete with all of the essentials, including cots, an oil stove, table, lanterns, and pans. All other provisions could be ordered daily from the camp store, pictured above, for delivery the next morning.

The canvas-walled tents, either 8 by 16 feet or 8 by 24 feet, had wood roofs and floors, front and back porches, and two windows facing the lake. Curtains separated the interior into two or three rooms, depending on the size of the tent. The accommodations appealed to those who wished to enjoy a camping vacation without completely "roughing it." As Kraus advertised, Camp Village made camping at Lake Hopatcong "inexpensive and practical," a philosophy he continued to follow at Bertrand Island.

CALIFORNIA LODGE, BERTRAND ISLAND, LAKE HOPATCONG, N.J.

Louis Kraus dreamed of operating a hotel on Lake Hopatcong. In 1919, he gave up teaching, acquired the property surrounding the beach at Bertrand Island, and built California Lodge. The hotel, seen here in 1922, faced out onto King Cove and was located across from what later became the entrance to Bertrand Island Park.

The hotel had 40 rooms and featured a dance hall, lively music, and numerous recreational activities. Rooms cost $16 per week. Tapping his previous experience in bringing convenience to vacationers, Louis Kraus built the hotel in a one-story horseshoe shape, and had each room open directly to the outside, allowing guests easy access to the bathing beach and other amusements. This photograph shows a masquerade ball in the California Lodge dance hall on August 3, 1920.

Being a neighbor to the bathing beach and the amusements, Kraus soon realized that there was more of a future in the amusement business than as a hotel owner. This 1919 photograph shows the dance hall at California Lodge on the left and the refreshment stand on the right.

California Lodge continued operating as a hotel until the mid-1920s. However, Louis Kraus began to turn his attention to the land adjoining the hotel. Kraus is seen here outside California Lodge with his daughter Dorothy Kraus and some friends in 1924.

When the beach at Bertrand Island was offered for sale in 1921, Louis Kraus and a partner, Charles Schleicher, acquired it. They now owned all of the land that was to constitute Bertrand Island Park. Seen above is the view across Bertrand Island's bridge looking toward the beach.

This was the lakefront at Bertrand Island as it appeared in 1921, when the beach was still operated by the Schoof family. After purchasing the beach, Louis Kraus built a boardwalk along the lake.

This photograph, taken in the autumn of 1921, shows workmen getting ready to build the wooden boardwalk, which was completed in time for the 1922 season. Over the years the boardwalk was changed from wood to asphalt, but it always was the equivalent of the park's midway.

The location of the boardwalk allowed concessions to be constructed in front of the hill, which stood on Bertrand Island, and to face out toward the lake. As seen in this c. 1922 photograph, Lacey's Photo Studio was one of the first concessions on the boardwalk.

The popularity of the beach brought visitors to Bertrand Island and allowed for the park's expansion. To serve the beach patrons, Louis Kraus built a row of 400 bathhouses for the 1922 season. Above, a photograph from that summer demonstrates why additional bathhouses were soon to be needed.

In the early years, Louis Kraus operated California Lodge and Bertrand Island Park as one. This *c.* 1924 photograph shows the Bertrand Island bus, which picked up customers at both Lake Hopatcong train stations. After California Lodge ended operations as a hotel, Kraus used its rooms for many years as living quarters for park workers and entertainers. The California Lodge dining hall remained as a catering facility for the park through the 1930s.

Four

A Bona Fide
Amusement Park

The 1920s were a period of tremendous growth for Bertrand Island Park and witnessed the arrival of many of the park's favorite attractions. While amusements were constantly added and removed as tastes changed over the years, the park's basic design and major rides changed little from this period. This 1925 photograph shows some happy visitors ready to embark on a boat tour from the park.

In March 1923, fire destroyed Bertrand Island's dance pavilion, as seen in this photograph. Louis Kraus immediately embarked on plans to build a new and much grander dance pavilion on the same site.

T-O-N-I-G-H-T
Grand Opening of New Dance Pavillion
at
Bertrand Island

Many Beautiful Prizes to be Given to the Ladies.   Novelties Galore.

Don't Miss This Event.   It will be the Biggest Thing to Happen at Lake Hopatcong This Season.

Quickly erected in time for opening in August 1923, the new June Rose Ballroom was a huge success for the park. In an era when dancing to the music of the big bands was *the* thing to do, the June Rose was quite the spot. Louis Kraus kept a steady stream of bands playing.

Seen here in 1924, the June Rose Ballroom was renamed Bertrand Island Villa in 1949. The building was used in later years as a restaurant, a lounge, and even as a venue for rock and roll concerts.

The June Rose Ballroom featured a 50- by 100-foot dance floor. The new building was considered fireproof, having been constructed of concrete and steel. Its attractive exterior was covered with stucco. Inside, even the ceiling was decorated. Although there was no air conditioning, patrons remember the dance floor as always having a nice cross-breeze through the open doors and windows.

Early on, Louis Kraus instituted an operating plan that proved to be one of the keys to the park's success. Rather than owning all of the amusements and stands, he began renting out spaces to concessionaires for rides, games, and refreshments. Seen here are two longtime concessionaires, Jack Weiner and Bill Hockenjos.

Kraus's policy resulted in concessionaires who stayed at the park for many, many years. Names such as Grant, Weiner, Hockenjos, Tirella, Bucci, Donofrio, Nazzaro, Mulvey, James, Moran, Schiavo, DeMarino, Pecoraro, and many others were well remembered by the park faithful.

Karl Woda, more popularly known as "Hot Dog Charlie," had a stand located on the front corner of the boardwalk, seen here in 1937.

Working at the park was often a family affair, as witnessed by this 1930s photograph showing several members of the Woda family. Over the years, many children literally grew up at the park, spending summers helping their parents with the family's concessions. Many families used the extra income to put children through college. "We didn't become millionaires, but we sure had fun" was the way one former concessionaire summed up her family's years at the park.

In 1923, a parking lot with space for 500 cars was built and daily bus service from Newark was introduced. Bus service from around the area became vital to the park's success during the 1920s and 1930s. The Basket Pavilion, seen above, was constructed in 1924.

The Basket Pavilion was an open-air cafeteria where visitors could bring their own food or buy snacks on the premises. Also in 1924, the parking lot was doubled to accommodate 1,000 cars. To welcome the growing auto business, a new entrance was built on Bertrand Island Road. The park now offered a shooting gallery, a carousel, skee ball, a pony run, a photograph studio, carnival games, rowboats, canoes, and "speedboats" for sightseeing. Special events and dances were held throughout the week.

In the early 1920s, Louis Kraus furnished boat transportation to Bertrand Island Park from around the lake. To help advertise the park during this period, he brought entertainers to private docks around the lake on Tuesdays and Fridays. This early 1920s photograph shows off the park's "speedboat."

In 1925, a long-term lease to operate the sightseeing boats was given to Bill Hockenjos, who ordered a new 40-foot tour boat to be built by Barnes Brothers of Lake Hopatcong. Hockenjos's boats, as seen in this c. 1930 photograph, became a favorite means for visitors to experience the excitement and beauty of Lake Hopatcong.

The year 1925 was one of incredible growth for the park. Although five major new rides were introduced, no event transformed the park more than the construction of the roller coaster. Begun during the winter of 1924–1925, the roller coaster was built by the Philadelphia Toboggan Company at a cost of over $50,000, using some 280,000 feet of lumber.

The roller coaster was specifically designed to address the narrow strip of land on which Bertrand Island Park was located. The ride was approximately three quarters of a mile long, contained nine dips, and had a loop back at the end 50 feet in diameter. Cars were pulled up the first hill (some 80 feet high) by a steel cable powered by a 75-horsepower electric motor and proceeded the rest of the way purely by gravity. The construction of a roller coaster gave Bertrand Island credibility as an amusement park.

During the first weekend of June 1925, 10,000 people crammed the park to test the new amusements. More than 150 of them were still in line when the roller coaster closed Saturday at midnight. The roller coaster immediately became the park's most popular ride, and it remained such throughout the park's history.

Bertrand Island's bridge was filled in during the roller coaster's construction. It would have been located at left in this photograph before the coaster was built. In this era before significant government regulation, the parking lot was expanded by filling in part of the lake. The new parking area could accommodate 2,500 automobiles. As part of this construction, the road from the park to the former island was straightened and relocated along the south shore, where it remains today.

Also opening for the 1925 season was the Whip, which became another longtime favorite at the park. The Whip consisted of two-person cars traversing an oval shaped course, which produced a whipping effect at each end. Twelve such rides survive today in the United States. Enthusiasts can still experience the Whip at nearby Playland in Rye, New York, and at Knoebel's, Dorney Park, and Bushkill Park, all in Pennsylvania.

The aeroplane swing, another ride introduced in 1925, featured six biplanes with propellers that actually turned. The ride was built next to the bathing beach and the planes swung out high over Lake Hopatcong. At the left in this c. 1930 photograph is the carousel house, and visible behind the swing is the Whip.

Also debuting in 1925 was the Rolling Waves, a ride described as similar to a merry-go-round but with a tipping-up-and-down motion as it revolved. During the Fourth of July weekend in 1925, more than 55,000 people were reported to have entered the park. Bertrand Island had become a bona fide amusement park.

In 1926, the popular bathing beach was made 300 feet longer. Added for this season were the electric scooters, or Dodgem bumper cars. The Dodgem's 15 cars were housed in a specially constructed building located to the left of the park's entrance.

The year 1926 also saw the boardwalk widened by ten feet, as seen in this late-1920s photograph. Visible are some of the advertised 10,000 electric bulbs that illuminated the park at night.

This late-1920s photograph witnesses the growth of the boardwalk.

The Philadelphia Toboggan Company was again at work at Bertrand Island in 1926, this time building the Old Mill. The ride, part tunnel of love and part thrill ride, had boats propelled along through a tunnel by water current. Construction required 39,440 feet of lumber and each of the eight boats cost $166.93. In 1939, the windmill above the Old Mill's entrance, visible in this photograph, was removed and the ride was renamed the Lost River.

This late-1920s photograph shows the entrance to the Old Mill on the left and the skee ball building at right. A new building for skee ball and billiards was erected in 1923 across from the dance hall near the park's entrance. In 1958, it was replaced by a new skee ball building in the same location.

The year 1926 also saw the debut of a new "water toboggan" at the bathing beach. During the 1920s and 1930s, Bertrand Island's beautiful sand beach was one of its most popular attractions. The diving float and water chute slides were favorites. Park visitors could change into bathing attire and even rent bathing suits in the Bathing Pavilion.

Bertrand Island's swimming area was a man-made beach that sloped very gradually until it reached the floating diving platform. Many a macho visitor was bailed out by the park's lifeguards, seen above c. 1930, after finding out that the water on the far side of the diving platform was very deep.

Bertrand Island's popular water slides are seen here during the 1930s. The Whip is visible in the background.

In a much less litigious era, diving was permitted from the upper levels of the diving platform, seen here in the 1930s.

The first carousel at Bertrand Island was a steam-powered model located off the beach during the 1910s. George Hulmes, center, had lost his business when the Bertrand Island Transportation Company's boats burned in the dance hall fire of March, 1923. In May, he erected a new merry-go-round house at the western edge of the park and purchased a carousel.

BERTRAND ISLAND PARK

will be open every day during

SEPTEMBER

All Rides and Games, as well as Dining Room, open during the day time from Mondays to Fridays and evenings on Saturdays and Sundays

- DANCING -

Every Saturday Evening and Sunday Afternoon and Evening during September

The management of Bertrand Island Park wishes to thank the people of Lake Hopatcong for it's patronage during the past summer and hopes that they have found this park the same high class and clean amusement center that the management has tried to make it.

Louis Kraus's management philosophy is evident in the last paragraph of this 1929 advertisement. He managed the park tightly to assure that it was run to his standards.

Five

GO WHERE
THE CROWD GOES

The 1920s were a period of both growth and competition for Bertrand Island. Its success with the roller coaster and other major rides led to the development of another amusement park on Lake Hopatcong. Ultimately, the park with the better management and ability to promote itself was to win out. During the 1920s, Louis Kraus supervised Bertrand Island Park's expansion. Following the onset of the Depression in October 1929, his attention shifted to overseeing the park's survival in the economic turmoil of the 1930s.

MENU

Nolan's Point Amusement Park

DINING ROOM

$1.50   *Regular Dinner* $1.50

Olives   Celery   Gherkins

SOUP
Consomme
Cream of Tomato   Chicken and Rice

CHOICE ROASTS
Choice Roast Milk Fed Chicken
Choice Roast Prime Ribs of Beef
Leg of Spring Lamb, Mint Jelly

Boiled New Potato   Garden Peas
Mashed Potatoes   Stringless Beans
Salad

DESSERTS
Assorted Pies
Cabinet Pudding   Baked Apple
Grape Fruit   Short Cake
Tea   Coffee   Postum   Milk   Cocoa

TO ORDER
STEAKS, CHOPS AND RAREBITS

Amusements had been present at the Nolan's Point section of Lake Hopatcong from the arrival of the first excursion trains there in the 1880s. By 1895, Nolan's Point had a merry-go-round (seen above *c.* 1910), a rifle gallery, and assorted games.

Following the demise of the large Nolan's Point icehouse in the early 1920s, amusements spread to the area between where the Jefferson House and Windlass restaurants are located today. In 1919, electric lighting was added and, by the late 1920s, Nolan's Point Amusement Park was in full competition with Bertrand Island.

Nolan's Point Amusement Park followed Bertrand Island with a roller coaster of its own, a Whip, an aeroplane swing, and other amusements. It constructed a sand beach and made full use of what was advertised as "New Jersey's largest picnic grove" to encourage group outings. The above photograph shows the Nolan's Point midway, c. 1925.

The electric scooter (or Dodgem) was also at Nolan's Point Amusement Park, along with a shooting gallery, a railroad, a pony track, a carousel, and games. In the 1930s, Nolan's Point Amusement Park followed the nation's big band craze and featured the music of Frank Daly and his Meadowbrook Orchestra in a dance pavilion that was advertised as having the capacity to seat 1,000.

During this period of competition with Nolan's Point, Louis Kraus aggressively marketed Bertrand Island. Location helped Kraus. Nolan's Point Amusement Park was largely dependent upon visitors arriving by train, whereas Bertrand Island could be easily accessed by road.

Unfortunately for Nolan's Point, automobiles were rapidly replacing trains as the preferred method of transportation. As the Central Railroad of New Jersey's train service to Nolan's Point declined, so did business at the park. With limited parking and poor road access, the park was not able to accommodate the growing automobile trade, as was Bertrand Island. To welcome the growing auto business, a new entrance (seen in this 1932 photograph) was built on Bertrand Island Road in 1924.

Another tremendous problem for Nolan's Point Amusement Park was the economy. As America struggled through the Depression, and some 75 percent of America's amusement parks were forced to close, it became apparent that Lake Hopatcong could not support two parks. Louis Kraus heavily marketed Bertrand Island, emphasized its positives (as seen in this 1930s advertisement) and assured its survival.

Nolan's Point Amusement Park went bankrupt in 1931, briefly reopened under new management, and closed for good in 1933. The name Nolan's Point Amusement Park continued to be associated with the site during the latter part of the 1930s, as groups still used the surviving picnic area and beach, and a roller rink which had opened. The roller coaster remained an imposing monument to the closed park, until it was finally dismantled in 1940. Meanwhile, Bertrand Island adapted to the new automobile trade, as seen in this 1932 photograph and, thanks to excellent promotions, was able to weather the Depression.

As depicted in this 1927 advertisement, Bertrand Island sought to draw people based on a combination of its location on a large lake with a sand beach, its many rides, and its large ballroom.

50

Varied entertainment was a key to drawing visitors to Bertrand Island. Here, a clown serenades Elsie Kraus, the wife of the park's owner.

GO WHERE THE CROWD GOES

BERTRAND ISLAND PARK

LAKE HOPATCONG'S LUNA PARK

DANCING To Tantilizing Music in the Most Gorgeous Ball Room in North Jersey.

FUN On the Thrilling Rides Along the Gay Boardwalk At the Sandy Bathing Beach

Whatever the current craze, Louis Kraus saw to it that it came to Bertrand Island. The park hosted such events as daredevils, fireworks, Vaudeville shows, amateur nights, swim championships, rocket boats, baby parades, movies, and benefits for many local causes. This 1928 advertisement compares the park to Coney Island's Luna Park.

The 1932 National Professional Marathon Swimming Championships were staged at Bertrand Island. A women's 5-mile swim featured a $250 first prize, and a men's 10-mile swim offered a $500 first prize. Laps measuring one-third mile were set up directly in front of the boardwalk

OFFICIAL PROGRAM

Men's Ten-Mile Event

OF THE

National Professional Marathon Swimming Championships

GEORGE YOUNG

AT

BERTRAND ISLAND PARK

LAKE HOPATCONG, N. J.

Saturday, July 9, 1932

PRICE 10 CENTS

THRILL OF THRILLS

MARVELO

BURNED ALIVE

Amazing-Sensational-Mysterious-Daring

Imagine, if you can, a human being enclosed in a metal casket in the middle of a huge, roaring bon-fire for over ten minutes. That is what you will witness at

Bertrand Island Park

ON LAKE HOPATCONG

FRIDAY, SATURDAY and SUNDAY EVENINGS

JUNE 28--29--30

FREE ∴ FREE ∴ FREE

FIREWORKS JULY 4th

IN THE BEAUTIFUL ROSE BALLROOM

CLIVE SHERMAN

AND HIS FAMOUS RIVIERA ORCHESTRA

EVERY MONDAY	EVERY THURSDAY
BARGAIN NITE	**GIFT NITE**

The year 1935 witnessed the daredevil Marvelo, who would enclose himself in an iron casket around which was placed flammable debris saturated with gasoline. The debris would then be ignited for 10 minutes, totally engulfing Marvelo in an inferno. At Bertrand Island, this was staged on a floating platform on the lake in front of the boardwalk.

A highlight of 1939 were "sky dancers" Betty and Benny, who performed all types of dances on a platform 18 inches in diameter, while atop a 150-foot pole, and with no net. In three shows a day during their week-long engagement at the park, the daring duo would perform such dances as the fox trot, waltz, and Charleston, not to mention skipping rope and dancing blindfolded.

Vaudeville shows in the June Rose Ballroom were a popular draw. As seen in this advertisement from 1931, the orchestra then appearing at the ballroom could be added right into the list of acts, with dancing following the show. During this period, Louis Kraus utilized the growing popularity of radio to publicize Bertrand Island, sponsoring the Milkman's Matinee, a radio show featuring the Bertrand Island Picnickers.

VAUDEVILLE

THURSDAY EVENING, JUNE 25th, 8:30 SHARP

DANCING FOLLOWS

5 BIG FEATURE ACTS 5

DAVE GARDNER
A LAUGH RACKETEER

PELOT & WILSON COMEDY JUGGLERS | | **FOLEY & MASON** BURLESQUE ACROBATS

MARY TITUS — Novelty Acrobatic Dancer

The Dancing McDonalds & Barbra Claire
THRILLING WHIRLWIND DANCERS

PAUL GRAHAM
AND HIS GRAHAM CRACKERS

NOW PLAYING   **TOMMY TUCKER**   AND HIS CALIFORNIANS

AT

BERTRAND ISLAND PARK

LAKE HOPATCONG

PERFECT SOUND

MOVIES

A LASS WHO LOVED SOLDIERS AND MARINES *until* **SHE LEARNED ABOUT SAILORS**

A FOX *Picture* with

LEW AYRES
ALICE FAYE

Produced by JOHN STONE

---ALSO---
BUSTER KEATON IN "ALLEZ OOP" AND "BEANS" A FUNNY CARTOON

PARK PLAN   **DANCING**   TO FOLLOW

AT

BERTRAND ISLAND PARK
LAKE HOPATCONG

WEDNESDAY EVENING, AUGUST 22

MOVIES AT 8:30 P. M.   DANCING AT 10 O'CLOCK

ADMISSION - - - - 25c

Movies were still a novelty, with sound having been introduced in 1928, and Bertrand Island featured films at various times during the 1930s (as seen in this 1934 advertisement). During 1937, movies were added as a regular Friday night attraction.

You Can Own a Complete Set
of Dinner Dishes
at no cost

by choosing TUESDAY EVENINGS *for your*

——GOOD TIMES AT——

Bertrand Island

HERE'S WHAT YOU DO

For every 10 cents you spend anywhere in the Park on any Tuesday Evening during the summer, between the hours of 8 P. M. and Midnight, you will receive a coupon. Ten (10) of these coupons entitles you to ONE piece of the set. No limit to the number of pieces you can take with you each night. Friends may pool their coupons and a fair sized group could take a complete set in one evening. If you have less than 10 coupons on any evening, they may be used on any following Tuesday.   :   :   :   :   :   :   :

No Raffles – No Lucky Numbers – No Waiting
You Receive According to Your Spending

See One of These
DINNER SETS on DISPLAY
in front of the Park Ball Room

FREE TALKING PICTURES *on every* FRIDAY
for Adults and Children at 8:30 P. M.

Giveaways became popular at many venues during the Depression and Bertrand Island was no exception, as witnessed by this 1937 advertisement.

Perhaps no event in Bertrand Island Park's history created more of a stir than the August 1937 appearance of Sally Rand, whose popularity had made her the highest-paid performer at the 1933 Chicago World's Fair. Performing her bubble dance and the fan dance that made her famous at the fair, Sally Rand left quite a lasting impression at Lake Hopatcong. Her act earned her $5,000 a week on the vaudeville circuits, quite a lofty sum in the 1930s.

Six

NEVER A DULL MOMENT

BERT NORMAN AND HIS
BERTRAND ISLAND ORCHESTRA

Throughout the 1920s and 1930s, the June Rose Ballroom was one of the park's most popular attractions, featuring an assortment of popular regional bands. During many years, the ballroom was even open throughout the off-season. Bert Norman and his Bertrand Island Orchestra were favorites during the 1924 and 1925 seasons and were broadcast live each Friday night from Bertrand Island.

The June Rose Ballroom featured nightly dancing during the season. Policies changed over the years, largely due to economics. In some years bands were rotated frequently, and in other years one band was hired for the entire season.

During this period, the ballroom had a "dime a dance" policy. Admission to the ballroom was 10¢. In addition, a container was placed near the entrance to the dance floor and dancers dropped their coins in as they stepped onto the floor. After a few songs, the dance floor was emptied. Those who wished to continue dancing had to pay another dime to reenter.

HARRY COX *and* HIS ORCHESTRA

During the 1920s, Bertrand Island advertised the "most beautiful pavilion at the lake with a ten piece orchestra." Among the popular bands of this period were Harry Cox and his orchestra.

Most bands lodged at the park while appearing at the ballroom. California Lodge, which ceased operating to the public *c.* 1925, housed such acts and the band members spent their days around the lake, as seen in this 1920s photograph.

During the 1930s, bands such as Jimmy Van Cleef and his Greenwich Village Orchestra, the Boys from Syracuse, Tommy Tucker and his Californians, and the Dan Gregory Orchestra filled the June Rose Ballroom. The quality entertainment in the ballroom, along with other promotions, helped attract patrons to the park during these tough economic times.

SONNY BOY   GOOFUS   CLEM "FAT" GORITY   MINNIE   MY FANNIE

WITH DAN GREGORY'S ORCHESTRA AT BERTRAND ISLAND PARK - LAKE HOPATCONG,

Bands often had a featured performer, such as Fat Gority, who mixed music and comedy. Playing at the park during the 1934 season with the Dan Gregory Orchestra, Gority was described as "one of dance-lands outstanding clowns." He appeared again at Bertrand Island in 1938 with Gill Crest and his Ohio Staters.

Among the popular acts to play at Bertrand Island was Walt Sears and his Dixies, a fairly well-known radio orchestra featuring swing music, which appeared at Bertrand Island in July 1939.

Appearing with the Walt Sears band was a 22-year-old singer from Steubensville, Ohio, performing under the name Dino Martini. In 1940, he shortened his stage name to Dean Martin.

Cottie Clark
and her
"GEORGETTES"
The Girl Sensation from the South

Assisted by
An ALL GIRL FLOOR SHOW

Playing Every Evening at

𝕭𝖊𝖗𝖙𝖗𝖆𝖓𝖉 𝕴𝖘𝖑𝖆𝖓𝖉 𝕻𝖆𝖗𝖐

Lake Hopatcong's Popular Amusement Center

Two Special Nights

On Every **MONDAY NITE** All Summer

10c
Admission to Ball Room
DANCING FREE
All Riding Devices (except boats) **5c**

On Every **THURSDAY NITE** All Summer

25c
Admission to Ball Room
DANCING FREE
25 Door Prizes Given Away **25c**

3

During the 1930s, Louis Kraus dropped the ballroom's "dime a dance" policy in order to attract patrons on days of the week that were traditionally slower. Instead, a small charge was collected to enter the ballroom and dancing was free. Cottie Clark and her Georgettes were an unusual all-girl band that played Bertrand Island in 1937.

The park's first Ferris wheel arrived in 1930 and quickly became a favorite way to view the lake. Also opening that year was a children's playground.

In 1931, public dock space was added, allowing lake residents to drive their own boats to the park. This photograph shows the view from the dock looking into the park.

LET 'EM DRIVE
JUST LIKE DADDY AT
BERTRAND ISLAND
LAKE HOPATCONG, N. J.
EVERYTHING FOR THE LITTLE ONES
Miniature Bathing Beach—Little Autos—Playground—
Picnic Grove—Thrilling Aeroplanes—Boat Rides
A WONDERFUL PICNIC PARK for MOTHERS and CHILDREN
Now Open
MOST ORIGINAL MINIATURE
GOLF COURSE IN THE STATE
Something Entirely Different
IN THE JUNE ROSE BALLROOM
EDDIE WORTH AND HIS COUNTY FAIR ORCHESTRA

A miniature auto speedway debuted in 1930 and served double duty as an outdoor roller-skating rink. This original track was located behind the Basket Pavilion.

The auto speedway was relocated several times over the years, with various types of miniature cars utilized. The earliest cars and speedway are seen above.

Bertrand Island Park always featured a selection of food at stands spread around the park. The popular Creamy Whip stand on the boardwalk featured soft ice cream.

Games of chance were associated with Bertrand Island from the beginning. Early games included a mouse game in which players tried to guess which hole a mouse would run into after being released. Other early games included a basketball throw and the Fish Pond, both of which remained virtually unchanged throughout the park's history.

A GREAT PLACE

——— FOR ———

KIDDIES

FROM SIX TO SIXTY

Lakeland's Own
PLAYGROUND

Bertrand Island Park

Lake Hopatcong

Thrilling Rides.   **Sandy Bathing Beach**

WONDERFUL VIEW OF LAKE
FROM OBSERVATION BOARDWALK

FREE DOCK FOR USE OF LAKE BOAT OWNERS
FREE AUTO PARKING ON WEEKDAYS

BIG VAUDEVILLE SHOW
EVERY FRIDAY EVENING
DANCING BEFORE AND AFTER THE SHOW

DANCING IN THE FAMOUS JUNE ROSE BALLROOM
THIRD BIG WEEK BY POPULAR DEMAND
CHARLES DORNBERGER and his VICTOR RECORDING ORCHESTRA

SPECIAL — WEDNESDAY EVENING — AUGUST 5TH
BATHING BEAUTY PAGEANTS
FOR SELECTION OF
"MISS BERTRAND ISLAND" ——and—— "LITTLE MISS LAKE HOPATCONG"

One of the few changes to the basic design of the park occurred in 1930 when the upper level of the park was developed. A series of small hills was removed and the land was graded to an elevation about 30 feet above lake level. This construction, planned before the Depression hit, gave the park room to introduce new attractions.

A second boardwalk was constructed on this upper section of the park. Adjacent to this upper or observation boardwalk was an impressive 18-hole miniature golf course, built to capitalize on the craze then sweeping the country.

As the July 26, 1930, edition of the *Lake Hopatcong Breeze* reported, "The miniature golf craze has hit Bertrand Island with a bang! . . . Everything from the putting greens to the tricky obstacles is entirely different from the many other miniature courses that dot the map hereabouts. The location on top of the observation hill is an ideal one, the cool breezes from the lake sweep it constantly."

In the upper portion of the park, by miniature golf, outdoor bowling was added in 1938. It consisted of regulation size alleys, as seen in this photograph of concessionaire Anne Woda, wife of "Hot Dog Charlie."

1. Some of the Riding Devices.
2. The famous Rose Ball-Room.
3. Gorgeous view from the Park.
4. Game Booths along Boardwalk.

Never a Dull Moment

1. BATHING — DANCING — FISHING
2. BOATING —
   Speed Boat Trips — Row Boats — Canoes
   — Sailing — U Drive Motorboats
3. RIDING DEVICES —
   Coaster — Dodgem — Old Mill — Rig a
   Jig — Miniature Autos and Railway —
   Carousel — Fun in the Dark — Airplane
   Swings — Whip
4. OUTDOOR GAMES —
   Bowling — Shuffle Board — Baseball —
   Golf Putting — Archery — Athletic Events
   — Swimming Contests
5. MIDWAY GAMES —
   Auto Race — Coney Race — Basketball
   — Fish Pond — Dart Game — Shooting
   Gallery — Grocery, Doll and Lamp
   Games — Whoopla — Walking Charlie
   — Arcade — Roll Down

Bertrand Island Park ~ the Ideal Picnic Spot

In 1929, Bertrand Island's first train ride was introduced. The little railroad was one-quarter mile long and circled the park, traveling along the lakeshore. The 1930s saw new attractions, such as archery; a parachute jump; Ride 'Em Cowboy, a mechanical bucking bronco; Drive Your Own Boats, 11-foot-long gasoline-powered boats in a walled channel in the lake; the Pretzel, later known as Fun in the Dark; Goofy House, later known as the Fun House; Rabbit Village, where visitors could view live rabbits inhabiting a miniature town; and a ride featuring small carts pulled by goats.

Elsie Kraus is pictured in front of the bathhouse, or bathing pavilion, where patrons changed into beach attire. For a small fee, clothes and belongings could be stored while guests enjoyed the beach.

The original rows of bathhouses, which existed during the beach's early years, became the more permanent structure seen below. In the late 1940s, this wooden building was replaced by a concrete structure, which existed until the park closed.

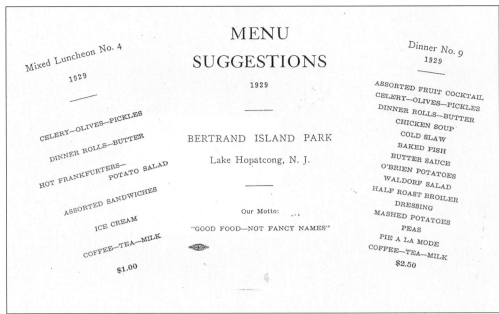

MENU
SUGGESTIONS

1929

BERTRAND ISLAND PARK

Lake Hopatcong, N. J.

Our Motto:

"GOOD FOOD—NOT FANCY NAMES"

Mixed Luncheon No. 4
1929

CELERY—OLIVES—PICKLES
DINNER ROLLS—BUTTER
HOT FRANKFURTERS—
POTATO SALAD
ASSORTED SANDWICHES
ICE CREAM
COFFEE—TEA—MILK

$1.00

Dinner No. 9
1929

ASSORTED FRUIT COCKTAIL
CELERY—OLIVES—PICKLES
DINNER ROLLS—BUTTER
CHICKEN SOUP
COLD SLAW
BAKED FISH
BUTTER SAUCE
O'BRIEN POTATOES
WALDORF SALAD
HALF ROAST BROILER
DRESSING
MASHED POTATOES
PEAS
PIE A LA MODE
COFFEE—TEA—MILK

$2.50

One of Louis Kraus's winning strategies for attracting customers was to market Bertrand Island aggressively for group outings, targeting company picnics as well as school and church trips.

Utilizing the June Rose Ballroom, the Dining Hall (originally part of California Lodge), and the Basket Pavilion, Louis Kraus could appeal to a wide cross section of groups with varied dining needs—from hot dogs to full dinners. Here, a group from Metropolitan Life Insurance Company gathers outside the Dining Hall in 1931.

Outings brought thousands of visitors at a time to Bertrand Island and introduced the park to new people, many of whom returned later with their families. The park enjoyed free publicity from the newspapers for larger outings, as witnessed by this coverage of the 1937 Loyalty Insurance outing.

Groups came from New York City, Connecticut, and all over northern New Jersey. In the photograph above, Warner Brothers employees enjoy their meal at the Dining Hall in 1935.

"The Ideal Picnic Rendezvous"

A Safe Bathing Beach for youngsters and those who cannot swim. The wate

A Sail of 14 miles on a beautiful lake.

Why BERTRAND IS

1. Lake Hopatcong is 9 miles long with 40 miles of shore and gorgeous scenery.
2. Beautiful Trip over good roads with little traffic.
3. No Admission Charge to the park at any time.
4. Free Basket Party Tables for nearly 4000 people.
5. Cafeteria for light lunches and refreshments.
6. Dining Hall seats 600 persons. Excellent Dinner for $1 served at all hours of the day.
7. Outing Banquets a specialty. Menus on request.
8. Drinking Water and clean, modern Comfort Stations are free.
9. Magnificent Ball Room and fine Dance Music.
10. Ten of the most popular Riding Devices and Games of many kinds.
11. Most excellent Bathing right in Lake Hopatcong in water pure enough to drink. Absolutely safe Beach. Bathers permitted to wander through the park in bathing attire.

LOUIS KRAUS, Manager   Phone Hopatcon

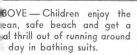

BOVE — Children enjoy the ean, safe beach and get a al thrill out of running around day in bathing suits.

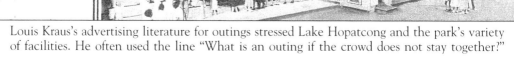

Louis Kraus's advertising literature for outings stressed Lake Hopatcong and the park's variety of facilities. He often used the line "What is an outing if the crowd does not stay together?"

72

LAKE HOPATCONG, N.J.

"The Mountain-Lake Paradise"

rink.

s so Popular

and Canoes to rent by the hour or day.

Boats for sight-seeing trips around the lake
of thrills.

amond free to outing parties.

tcong is about 1000 feet above sea-level,
temperature in its vicinity about 10 de-
r than in lower elevations and the cities.

ds clean, well-gardened and policed.

so designed that, while it covers about 30
bers of outing parties are kept in contact
other. There is not that "disbanding" that
at most other resorts after getting out of
busses. WHAT IS AN OUTING IF THE
OES NOT STAY TOGETHER? This point
d by those who have run outings to Bertrand
as one of the park's most valuable features.

Address: Lake Hopatcong, N. J.

ABOVE—The Basket
Pavilion, seating 500
persons, is FREE.

RIGHT — Cafeteria
where light lunches
and refreshments
are served to pic-
nickers.

LEFT—Dining Hall for
outing banquets, seat-
ing 600 persons. Ban-
quet Menus upon re-
quest. $1. Dinners
served all day to auto
parties.

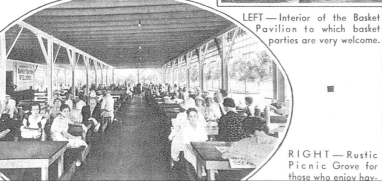

LEFT — Interior of the Basket
Pavilion to which basket
parties are very welcome.

RIGHT — Rustic
Picnic Grove for
those who enjoy hay-

emphasizing that although Bertrand Island had much to offer, it was small enough so that
groups did not get separated.

73

PASSAIC DAILY HERALD OUTING

SUNDAY, AUGUST 26, 1923

PASSAIC HERALD
OUTING
LAKE HOPATCONG

DANCING

BANANAS

HOT DOGS

SODA
ICE CREAM

BERTRAND ISLAND PARK
LAKE HOPATCONG, N. J.

Located on the park's westernmost boundary was a picnic grove that was perfect for outings of groups who wished to include traditional picnic events, such as three-legged races, baseball, and sack races. The picnic grove also gave groups a place to enjoy kegs of beer away from the main park. Part of this land was sold in the 1950s, and three houses were erected on the lakefront footage.

Perhaps no day was more memorable than August 2, 1929, when 130 buses brought 6,000 employees of the Wright Aeronautical Corporation from Paterson to Bertrand Island. The line of buses was 4 miles long. After every tenth bus was an extra bus to take care of possible breakdowns or emergencies. As an additional precaution, three wreckers also accompanied the caravan.

GEORGE and LILY GARDEN

—— Xylophone Wizards ——

REQUEST THEIR LAKE HOPATCONG FRIENDS
TO VISIT THEM AT THE

"OLD FASHIONED BEER GARDEN"

at

BERTRAND ISLAND PARK

Lake Hopatcong's Center of Amusement

The Gardens are the feature entertainers at the new beer garden at the Island. His friends know how George can play the accordion and piano, and the xylophone duets of George and Lily are a sensation.

THE FINEST DRAUGHT BEER   -   -   -   AT 10¢ A GLASS

Following the end of Prohibition in 1932, the park introduced a beer garden for the 1933 season featuring draft beer at 10¢ a glass. It was located in part of the old California Lodge and offered various types of entertainment.

The above photograph shows the 1935 West Side Boss Bakers Bowling League outing, which apparently was held at the beer garden.

In addition to concessionaires, the park directly employed maintenance and cleanup personnel. Lifeguards worked for the bathing beach concession. First aid personnel were on the premises, and a doctor was close by, if needed.

The park worked closely over the years with the Mount Arlington police department. Regular Mount Arlington police officers or specials who were employed on a part-time basis provided for the security needs of the park.

Lifeguarding at Bertrand Island Park was a great summer job but could be quite busy because of the popularity of the beach and the number of patrons without swimming experience. Pictured is a member of the 1929 lifeguard staff.

A joint security and first aid office was originally located near the roller coaster (seen here in the 1930s). The first aid office later moved into the administration building located by the park entrance.

WPA FEDERAL THEATRE PROJECT

FEDERAL THEATRE REVUE ★★★★

CAST of **40**

Dancers !
Singers !
Comedians !

Accompanied by a 14-pc. Orchestra

TUESDAY

Aug. 3

AT 8:30 P. M.

ADMISSION 40c

FREE DANCING After the Show to Jack Bryson and His Orchestra

— UNDER THE AUSPICES OF —

Bertrand Island Park

"Blue Monday Banished"

Every Monday is Bargain Nite

— AT —

Bertrand Island Park

Lake Hopatcong's Center of Amusement

Admission to Ball Room 15c   Dancing all Evening Free

All Riding Devices (except boats) - 5c

Cap't Sam's   SPEED BOAT SERVICE

Provides Bargain Boat Transportation To
BERTRAND ISLAND PARK

25c Every Monday Nite **25c**
Round Trip Fare

Fast Dependable Service

Speedboats Leave Following Docks Between 7 and 9 P. M.

| ELLSWORTH DOCK | SUNNYSIDE | LAKEVIEW |
| GREAT COVE | PLAYHOUSE PARK | KAY'S HOTEL |

The Federal Theatre Project was an effort by the Roosevelt Administration to provide work for unemployed theater professionals during the Depression. The project operated many theatrical companies throughout the United States from 1935 to 1939 and is credited with staging some of the most innovative productions of the day. It was a treat when the Federal Theatre Project teamed with Bertrand Island Park to present the above production in 1937.

Throughout the Depression, Louis Kraus sought to make the park a welcome relief to the dismal times. Happiness was the theme of advertisements, and reduced prices were a major advertising strategy. Also mentioned in the advertisement at the left is the boat transportation offered to the park during the 1930s by Sam Goodman of Nolan's Point, who operated large speedboats.

HEY KIDDIES ! ! !

DO YOU WANT TO DIG FOR

BURIED TREASURE

AT BERTRAND ISLAND PARK

LAKE HOPATCONG, N. J., on

FRIDAY EVENING, JULY 13TH

You'll find lots of pennies, nickles and dimes and some larger coins, besides coupons good for ice cream, soda, free rides on the merry-go-round, coaster, etc., as well as valuable prizes of all kinds.

READ THIS COUPON NOW

This coupon, when presented by a child under 12 years of age, will permit that child to enter the

TREASURE CAVE AT BERTRAND ISLAND PARK

and remove a bucket of sand from the massive treasure chest. Everything found in that bucket of sand will be the property of the child. **THIS COUPON IS GOOD ONLY ON**

FRIDAY EVENING, JULY 13th

or the following Friday, between the hours of 8 and 9 P. M.

Bring This Coupon With You

ONLY ONE COUPON ACCEPTED FROM EACH CHILD

COURTESY — BERNARDSVILLE NEWS

In 1932, in an effort to combat the tough economic times, Bertrand Island introduced reduced admission nights on Mondays and "Lucky Nights" on Thursdays, featuring prize giveaways. "Dollar dinners" became a regular feature, as did reduced admission nights at the ballroom. In addition, on Mondays all rides were reduced to 5¢. In 1934, the park introduced 3¢ rides for children; "Copper Miners Nights," during which children could dig for pennies; and a "Buried Treasure" game, in which coins of all values could be found.

The story of Bertrand Island's beloved carousel begins in the early 1920s, when a magnificent carousel was carved by the firm of Marcus C. Illions & Sons of Coney Island, New York. Only three such machines were completed by Illions and his staff. Considered one of the master carvers, Illions produced horses known for their wild expressions and glitzy trappings, which featured an abundance of gold leaf and colorful jewels. The newly carved carousel was sold to an amusement department store (seen above) on Surf Avenue in Coney Island.

At Coney Island, the Illions Monarch II Supreme carousel was known as the "Bobs Round About" and operated underneath a roller coaster. In 1937, Louis Accommando purchased the carousel in exchange for $7,200 and a smaller carousel. He moved his new purchase to the existing carousel house at Bertrand Island Amusement Park, where it remained as a landmark for the next 35 years.

Seven

THERE SHE IS

The introduction of beauty pageants to Bertrand Island was one of Louis Kraus's most successful promotions. While Lake Hopatcong's first beauty pageants were held at Nolan's Point in 1924, they made their debut at Bertrand Island in 1926 and thereafter became a regular feature of summer life at Lake Hopatcong. Regularly scheduled pageants remained a fixture at Bertrand Island until World War II.

During the 1920s and 1930s, beauty pageants were popular summer events across the nation. To capitalize on their popularity, Louis Kraus (seen below at the far right) developed a concept in 1927 that served the park well for many years. First, the park would hold a Miss Bertrand Island contest. Then, a few weeks later, the winner of that contest would compete in a second pageant against contestants representing hotels and other lake institutions for the coveted title of Miss Lake Hopatcong.

Bathing Beauty Contest

Bertrand Island Park

July 1, 1927, 8:30 P. M.

To Select "MISS BERTRAND ISLAND"

On July 1st at 8 P. M. the Management of Bertrand Island Park will stage a Bathing Beauty Contest in the Ballroom of the Park, for the purpose of selecting "Miss Bertrand Island."

"Miss Bertrand Island" will later (July 15th) represent the island in the big beauty contest to be staged by the Lake Hopatcong Association, also at the park pavilion. At this latter contest, "Miss Lake Hopatcong" will be selected.

"Miss Lake Hopatcong" will go to the Atlantic City Pageant in September. All her expenses will be paid by the Lake Hopatcong Association, including clothes. She will be chaperoned by two ladies of good character. This trip to Atlantic City, as a beauty contestant is a very interesting experience, and the lucky girl will surely enjoy it.

The Management of the Island will present to the winner of the contest, on July 1st, ("Miss Bertrand Island") a Jantzen bathing suit and a beautiful evening dress to be worn on July 15th, after which this will become her personal property.

The clothes presented by the Hopatcong Association will also become the property of the winner of the contest on July 15th, so, besides the pleasure and honor of winning the beauty contest, and the trip to Atlantic City, the fortunate young lady will have acquired a beautiful wardrobe. It is worth trying for, and any unmarried girl in any town in the vicinity of Lake Hopatcong is qualified.

Get an application blank at the Park office or the bathing pavilion for further particulars. Only thirty applications will be accepted, so do not delay your entry.

THE MANAGEMENT,

BERTRAND ISLAND PARK.

Beauty pageants provided much free publicity for Bertrand Island. Announcements of the contests were featured in local newspapers, and photographs of the winners were sure to receive coverage, often making it into the New York City press. The park attracted large crowds for the contests, and most attendees spent money on food and rides while there.

For a few years, a third contest was held at the end of the season in which Miss Lake Hopatcong would compete in a regional Miss North Jersey Lakes contest.

Margaret Eckdal, right, Miss America 1930, appeared at Bertrand Island that year to present the Miss Bertrand Island trophy to Helena Eklund of Wharton.

WEDNESDAY, AUGUST 20th

WILL BE A BIG DAY AT

Bertrand Island Park

LAKE HOPATCONG, N. J.

AFTERNOON AND EVENING—AUGUST 20th

"MISS AMERICA" of 1930
(MISS MARGARET EKDAHL)

will appear in person, wearing the bathing creations and beautiful evening gowns in which she will compete with the world's beauties at Rio De Janiero, South America, in September.

AFTERNOON AT 3 O'CLOCK—AUGUST 20th

"LITTLE MISS LAKE HOPATCONG"
A MINIATURE BATHING BEAUTY CONTEST

Note — Any Little Miss from 6 to 10 years of age may enter. Phone Hopatcong 136 for particulars.

EVENING AT 8 O'CLOCK—AUGUST 20th

"MISS BERTRAND ISLAND"
BATHING BEAUTY CONTEST

For the selection of the Young Lady to represent Bertrand Island Park at the "Miss Lake Hopatcong"

Contest to be held on the following Wednesday evening

Note — Any Young Lady between the ages of 16 and 24 may enter. Phone Hopatcong 136 for particulars.

"MISS AMERICA" of 1930

IN THE JUNE ROSE BALLROOM——TWO WEEKS COMMENCING MONDAY, AUGUST 11th

"DAN MURPHY and his MUSICAL SKIPPERS"

Celebrity appearances arranged by Louis Kraus helped bring additional people into the park. The 1930 Miss Bertrand Island pageant also featured a children's pageant during the day.

Contestants sometimes paraded along the lake, but most pageants were held at night in the June Rose Ballroom.

National Beauty PAGEANT

FOR THE SELECTION OF

"MISS AMERICA"

—AT—

Bertrand Island Park

on beautiful Lake Hopatcong

"MISS CONNECTICUT"
One of the 40 picked beauties
to compete for the title
"Miss America"

2 Gala Nites 2

TUES., AUGUST 28th
FASHION PARADE AND ELIMINATIONS
to select the 20 most beautiful Bathing
Beauties for Wednesday's finals.

WED., AUGUST 29th
FINAL BATHING BEAUTY CONTEST
Selection of "Miss America"

40 Gorgeous girls from various states and cities in a colorful pageant of pulchritude for the nation's highest beauty honors.

NOTE—Limited reserved seating capacity. Order seats early to avoid disappointment. Call at Park Office or phone Hopatcong 136.

Lake Land News 4 Dover, New Jersey

The biggest pageant held at Lake Hopatcong took place in 1934. The Miss America Pageant originated in Atlantic City in 1921, but due to financial problems and scandals concerning the eligibility of contestants, there were several years during the late 1920s and early 1930s when the contest was not held by the Atlantic City organization. This left the door open for other cities to hold the pageant, although these are not recognized today by the Miss America Organization. In 1934, young women from all over the country descended on Bertrand Island for a contest billed as Miss America 1934.

The Miss America 1934 pageant drew large crowds and was widely covered in the newspapers and newsreels. Miss Lake Hopatcong served as the hostess but, as was traditional during this time for the hosting city, was not allowed to compete. The winner was Myrtle Richardson, left, of Ardmore, Pennsylvania, who entered as Miss Millbourne. The event was a great public relations success for Bertrand Island.

Following a third-place finish in 1936, 17-year-old Bette Cooper of Hackettstown won the Miss Bertrand Island Pageant in July 1937. In August of that year, she won the Miss Lake Hopatcong pageant and traveled to compete in Atlantic City.

During these early years, the Miss America Pageant operated differently from the way it does today. Rather than have a representative from each state, organizations throughout the country were sanctioned by the Miss America Organization to hold contests and send their winners directly to Atlantic City. Such was the case with Bertrand Island. The winner of the Miss Lake Hopatcong contest went directly to compete in the Miss America Pageant, with her travel costs paid by the park. For publicity purposes, she competed as Miss Bertrand Island.

On September 11, 1937, Bette Cooper was named Miss America 1937. Surprised by the public appearances and schedule that Miss America was expected to meet, the overwhelmed winner disappeared for some 24 hours and the news services had a field day reporting that she had run off with her chaperone. Newspapers ran photographs showing the empty throne.

When the dust settled, Bette Cooper and her family demanded and received a less rigorous schedule than the Miss America Pageant officials had expected of the winner. This led to permanent changes in the rules for Miss America pageants. In 1938, Bette Cooper returned to Bertrand Island as Miss America to crown the 1938 Miss Lake Hopatcong.

Bertrand Island Amusement Park continued its close ties with beauty pageants, being selected to host the 1939, 1940, and 1941 Miss New Jersey pageants, with the winner being the state's sole representative in the Miss America Pageant. During these years, Bertrand Island held two contests each year, with the winner of the Miss Bertrand Island contest competing for the title of Miss New Jersey. Although no one knew it at the time, 1941 turned out to be the park's last beauty pageant, as World War II forced profound changes on the park.

Eight
CHANGE IS IN THE AIR

Louis Kraus owned Bertrand Island Park for almost 30 years, and the park developed and grew under his guidance. However, with the coming of World War II and the vastly changed America that followed, Bertrand Island had to adapt to America's new tastes and attitudes, and confront its single biggest social change: the baby boom. Above, Kraus's grandson Alan Cuda and friend Evelyn Craney get ready for a day of fun at the park in 1954.

When Bertrand Island Park closed for the season in September 1941, no one realized that America would be at war in just three months. With large numbers of local residents entering military service or working at Picatinny Arsenal and Hercules Powder, the good times associated with Lake Hopatcong gave way as the lake, along with the rest of the country, joined the war effort.

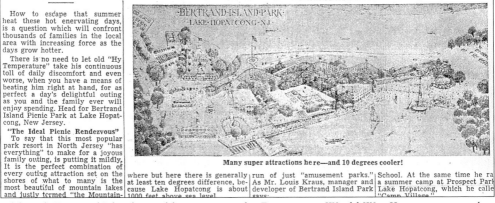

THE PATERSON MORNING CALL, FRIDAY, JULY 17, 1942

For Joyous Outing On 4 Gallons Gas Round Trip

How to escape that summer heat these hot enervating days, is a question which will confront thousands of families in the local area with increasing force as the days grow hotter.

There is no need to let old "Hy Temperature" take his continuous toll of daily discomfort and even worse, when you have a means of beating him right at hand, for as perfect a day's delightful outing as you and the family ever will enjoy spending. Head for Bertrand Island Picnic Park at Lake Hopatcong, New Jersey.

"The Ideal Picnic Rendezvous"

To say that this most popular park resort in North Jersey "has everything" to make for a joyous family outing, is putting it mildly. It is the perfect combination of every outing attraction set on the shores of what to many is the most beautiful of mountain lakes and justly termed "the Mountain-

Many super attractions here—and 10 degrees cooler!

where but here there is generally at least ten degrees difference, because Lake Hopatcong is about 1000 feet above sea level

run of just "amusement parks." As Mr. Louis Kraus, manager and developer of Bertrand Island Park says:

School. At the same time he ra a summer camp at Prospect Par Lake Hopatcong, which he calle "Camp Village."

Although Bertrand Island was able to survive the Depression, World War II was quite another story. The park remained open during the war, but many of the amusements were closed or remained very quiet. By law, lights had to be dimmed or turned off at night. The rationing of gasoline greatly limited automobile traffic to the lake. The park tried to attract customers in 1942, as seen in this newspaper clipping, but its distance from the cities greatly hindered its ability to entice wartime customers.

In 1948, still feeling the effects of the Depression and the financial suffering of the war years, Louis Kraus decided to sell the park to Lorenzo D'Agostino, son Ray D'Agostino, and Larry Donofrio, who were concessionaires under Kraus. Recognizing the value of his experience, the new owners asked Kraus to continue to help manage the park, which he did until his death in 1955.

Under the new leadership, the park began to evolve to reflect postwar attitudes. Bertrand Island concentrated more on amusements and games and less on special events. Ray D'Agostino became the park manager for the new team. Following his father's death in the late 1960s and Larry Donofrio's decision to sell his share shortly thereafter, Ray D'Agostino became sole owner of the park and remained so until 1978.

This map shows the park as it appeared c. 1940. The park changed little in basic design from the mid-1920s. The boardwalk located along the lake featured the penny arcade and many of the park's games. Behind the games was a hill leading to the park's upper section, known originally as the upper or observation boardwalk. (This area was renovated after World War II.) The carousel was at the park's western edge. Beyond the carousel was an open area used as a baseball field, picnic grove, and the overflow parking lot. Automobiles entered on Bertrand Road from the east. California Lodge can be seen to the extreme left. The Dining Hall, just above it, was removed to make room for more parking during the 1940s. Boat parking, originally allowed at one long dock, was replaced by individual docks in 1949. Except for those arriving by boat, visitors entered the park past the Dodgem and the June Rose Ballroom (listed as "Dance Hall" on this map).

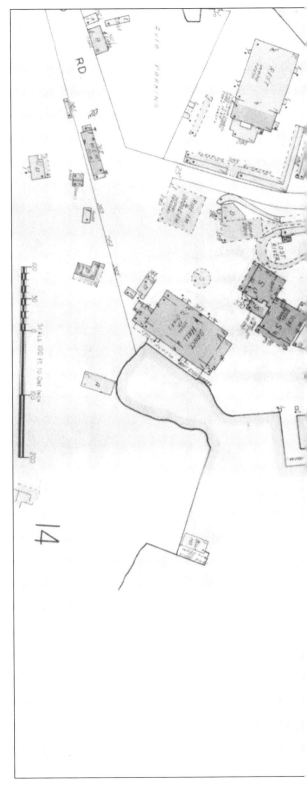

LAKE HOPATCONG VACATION & OUTING CO. INC.
AMUSEMENT PARK

95

As postwar Lake Hopatcong evolved from a hotel resort to an area of second homes and bungalows, Bertrand Island remained a popular place at which to enjoy a "day in the country," featuring its wonderful sand beach on New Jersey's largest lake. This early-1960s photograph demonstrates the beach's continued popularity.

With the hardships of World War II, many of the park's attractions fell into disrepair, and several rides left the park. The new owners addressed this situation in the late 1940s and early 1950s by undertaking major renovations and a redevelopment of the upper boardwalk area. New rides were added, as well as batting cages and a new miniature golf course.

One of the most popular postwar additions was Kiddieland, which made its debut at Bertrand Island in 1951. It was built on the site of the former Fun House, which had been a walk-through attraction featuring slides, mirrors, revolving barrels, and other obstacles.

Kiddieland featured rides scaled solely for children. These rides were particularly popular on Nickel Nights. The photographs here and on the next three pages were part of a publicity shoot done in 1954. It featured Louis Kraus's grandson Alan Cuda and Evelyn Craney (whose mother operated the root beer and french fry concession) enjoying some of the park's most popular attractions.

From its construction as the Old Mill in 1926, the Lost River remained a favorite until the park closed. There are seven Old Mills still in existence in the United States and two in the United Kingdom. However, most no longer feature a drop into water at the end of the ride. The closest Old Mills can be found at Playland in Rye, New York, and Nickels Midway Pier in Wildwood.

The bumper cars first made their appearance at the park in 1925 and were initially called "electric scooters." The cars were changed several times over the years, but the ride remained in the same building by the park entrance.

The penny arcade was a mainstay of the boardwalk for almost the entire life of the park. It featured a wonderful selection of vintage games, along with the latest fads such as Pacman and Air Hockey.

The "high striker" was located at the eastern end of the boardwalk. As seen in this photograph, the original prize for ringing the bell was a "good cigar."

The beach continued to be a main attraction in the postwar years, setting Bertrand Island aside from other northern New Jersey amusement parks that offered pools. In the park's later years, its beach was one of only two public ones on Lake Hopatcong (the other being Hopatcong State Park).

Food was available from individual concessions at various locations in the park. Rather than have all stands sell the same items, each food concession was largely unique.

Most of the park's games were located in a row along the boardwalk. Many of the games remained unchanged for years. Favorites included the basketball throw, Walking Charlies (Knock Their Hats Off), and the Fish Pond. The Greyhound Race, seen here, started out as a rabbit race.

There were several different wheels of fortune at the park. Over the years, patrons could attempt to win everything from bags of groceries to cigarettes to parakeets. The Bird Cage, seen below, was on the boardwalk in the early 1960s.

In the postwar years, outings continued to play a key role in the park's success. Ray D'Agostino actively marketed the park to school, church, and camp groups, as well as to companies for outings. The park continued to feature the idea that the layout of the park allowed groups to stay together.

Buses were the lifeblood of the park, particularly on weekdays. On a normal weekday, dozens of buses would come to at the park. One of the park's largest outings occurred in August 1952, when it hosted some 7,000 Picatinny Arsenal employees.

Bertrand Island Villa Menu

Grapefruit Juice	.15	Tomato Juice	.15
Orange Juice	.15	Fruit Cup	.25

◆ ◆

Tomato Soup	.25	Chicken Rice Soup	.25

◆ ◆

Broiled T-Bone Steak, French Fries, Lettuce and Tomato	2.75
Veal Cutlet Pamegan with Spaghetti	2.75
Roast Turkey, Dressing, Potatoes, Vegetable	2.00
Roast Sirloin of Beef, Potatoes, Vegetable	2.00
Chopped Sirloin Steak, Potatoes, Vegetable	1.50
Southern Fried Chicken, French Fries	1.50
Half Broiled Chicken, French Fries and Vegetable	1.75
Italian Spaghetti and Meat Balls	1.25
Italian Spaghetti with Tomato Sauce	1.00
Pizza Pie	1.35
To Take Out	1.50
Pizza Pie with Anchovies	1.50

◆ ◆

Rice Pudding	.15	Jello	.15
Ice Cream	.15	Assorted Pies	.20
	Deep Dish Apple Pie	.25	
Coffee or Tea	.10 Milk	.15 Iced Tea	.20

◆ ◆

Special Turkey Dinner - - - $2.50

Fruit Cup or Juice
Soup
Roast Turkey and Dressing
Mashed Potatoes   Vegetable
Cole Slaw
Ice Cream or Pie
Coffee, Tea or Milk

◆ ◆

Hot Sandwiches

Roast Turkey with French Fried Potatoes and Gravy	1.25
Roast Sirloin of Beef with French Fried Potatoes and Gravy	1.25

Cold Sandwiches

Sliced Polish Ham	.60	Ham and Swiss Combination	.60
American Cheese	.35	Lettuce and Tomato	.40
Tuna Fish	.50	Chicken Salad	.60
Bacon, Lettuce and Tomato	.60	Spiced Ham and Lettuce	.50
Sliced Cold Turkey	.85	Club Sandwich	1.00
Imported Swiss Cheese	.50	Cold Roast Beef	.85

Salads

Tuna Fish Salad	1.25	Combination Vegetable Salad	1.00
Sardine Salad	1.25	Shrimp Salad	1.50
Hard Boiled Egg Salad	1.00	Cold Cuts and Potato Salad	1.50

Under the new park ownership, the June Rose Ballroom was renamed Bertrand Island Villa. Its main function shifted from an entertainment venue to a restaurant, and it was used heavily for group outings and banquets. As evidenced by this mid-1950s menu, the Villa offered a varied selection at reasonable prices. The Basket Pavilion continued to cater to groups that wished to bring bag or picnic lunches.

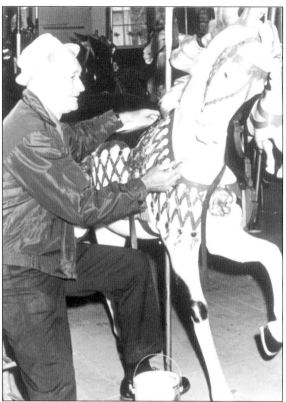

Upon Louis Accommando's death in 1960, the Illions carousel passed to his nephew and niece. They soon sold the carousel to their younger brother, Joe DeLorenzo, left, who had been running it for them. DeLorenzo and his wife Nelle DeLorenzo lovingly operated the carousel at Bertrand Island for the next decade. Along with 48 carved horses, it featured two lion chariots, a 165-note B & B band organ, and brass rings.

In 1972, a new amusement park being developed in Orlando, Florida, was seeking a special carousel. After meeting with Joe DeLorenzo, Circus World purchased the carousel for what was considered an enormous price at the time: $68,000. A smaller, undistinguished carousel, seen above, replaced the Illions and operated in the original carousel building.

The exquisite Illions Supreme underwent an extensive two-year restoration before thrilling Circus World patrons, including the visiting Joe DeLorenzo, seen here riding the carousel's lead horse. After Circus World closed in 1985, the carousel was set to return to New Jersey with a Weehawken developer. Unfortunately, the deal fell through. In 1988, the Illions Supreme was auctioned off, horse by horse, a fate that befell many carousels during this period, as collectors began to pay heavily for individual figures, prompting ride owners to break up their machines.

Individual horses from Bertrand Island's Illions carousel have since been resold at amounts over $100,000. The carousel base, without any horses but with its extremely ornate carving, was recently sold to a restaurant in Pasadena, California, which hopes to have it refitted and put back into use. Meanwhile, trim from the carousel is being displayed there.

The concept of reduced prices for rides was introduced at Bertrand Island during the Depression. By 1938, Monday night had become known as bargain night, Thursday as prize night, and Friday as Nickel Night. This evolved into the Nickel Nights or Bargain Nights that remained a popular feature at the park long after the Depression ended. In 1950, the park settled on Mondays and Thursdays as Nickel Nights.

Nickel Nights provided a tremendous boost in attendance on Mondays and Thursdays and forever endeared the park to thousands of youngsters who arrived with a dollar or two and kept busy all night. During the 1950s and 1960s, it was common for an adult to fill the car with neighborhood kids or for a parent to drop off children and pick them up later. This aerial photograph shows the park as it appeared in 1965.

The redevelopment of the upper boardwalk area in the 1950s included the addition of several new rides including the Moon Rocket, Tilt-A-Whirl, Tub O' Fun, and a new train ride.

The roller coaster continued as the park's most popular ride. As is the nature of wooden roller coasters, it had a unique sway that terrified some riders and thrilled others. The roller coaster required constant maintenance and was not without controversy, suffering a major fire in 1970, a collision in 1973, and numerous injuries that usually occurred when passengers stood up while the ride was in progress.

The original miniature golf course of the 1930s had occupied a major portion of the upper boardwalk. The park's new miniature golf course, pictured at the left, opened in the 1950s. Nestled between the batting range and the roller coaster, the new course did not offer a view of the lake, as the original one had. Also, it was smaller; but it was still an interesting course.

The new train ride of the 1950s had a much smaller layout than that of the original train, which actually had circled the park. Geared mostly to children, the new ride was located close to Kiddieland and traveled in a circle around the upper portion of the park.

In the late 1950s, the six biplanes of the aeroplane swing were replaced by three silver rocket ships, which had been acquired from Olympic Park, an amusement park located on the Maplewood-Irvington border.

The Aero-jets, as they were now called, were some 20 feet long and had four rows of seats. Seated in the third row of the Aero-jet is park co-owner Lorenzo D'Agostino, enjoying the ride with his granddaughter. At the lower left is the whale ride of the 1960s, in which riders could drive small, colorful, fiberglass whale-shaped boats powered by car batteries around an established route in Lake Hopatcong.

As boat taxi service waned at Lake Hopatcong, individual docks were added in 1949 for the increasing number of patrons who wished to arrive by private boat. Other changes under Ray D'Agostino's leadership included the addition of roller-skating in 1951. Roller-skating was first located next to skee ball and then moved into the Villa, before being phased out.

Fun in the Dark was a "dark ride" in which patrons boarded a small car and were taken through a building full of items meant to be scary. At various places, the car made sudden turns. The ride was originally opened as the Pretzel in 1930.

By the 1950s and 1960s, Lake Hopatcong had become similar to some of today's New Jersey shore towns, with second homes and weekly, monthly, and seasonal rental properties prevalent. Bertrand Island remained a highlight of any visit to the lake.

Bill Hockenjos operated the boat concession until 1957, when he sold to the Orth family. The Orths operated the boats until 1970. Boats such as the *Maggie and Jiggs,* which had been built at Barnes Brothers Marina on Lake Hopatcong, gave way to newer boats built at the Jersey Shore. One surviving boat from the park was last known to be operating at a park in Pennsylvania.

The Fish Pond was a favorite of many a young visitor, as every player won a prize. Prizes matched the number of the metal fish "hooked" by the magnet on the end of a fishing pole. This game was present for almost the entire duration of the park.

The shooting gallery, another an old favorite at the park, was located near the bathing beach by the ramp that led to the upper portion of the park. It featured Remington 22-caliber "gallery special" guns that fired a short round which turned into powder when it struck a target.

Boardwalk games remained popular, although prizes changed to match the tastes of the day. Over the years, games offered prizes such as groceries, cigarettes, kewpie dolls, lamps, candy, goldfish, and birds.

Whether it was caramel corn, cotton candy, pizza, hot dogs, or ice cream, one did not have to walk far to cure a case of the "munchies" at Bertrand Island. The large snack bar pictured here was located across from the beach.

This hamburger and hot dog stand was located at the front corner of the boardwalk, down the stairs from the park's entrance.

The Creamy Whip stand was located near the middle of the boardwalk, across from the penny arcade.

This is the same stand as above, but the "creamy whip" theme has been updated.

This snack stand was located outside of skee ball, near the entrance to the roller coaster.

A later addition across the boardwalk from the main row of games was a stand-alone concession housing a second shooting game. Contestants attempted to shoot out the entire star from a piece of paper.

Kiddieland remained relatively unchanged from its debut in 1951 until the park closed. Rides included cars, boats and helicopters . . .

flying fish, and fire trucks.

When Ray D'Agostino began managing the park, the only ride by the park entrance was the Dodgem. In the 1950s, the Boomerang was added next to the Villa. A unique, possibly one-of-a-kind ride, the Boomerang had to be manually operated, and was a favorite ride for many.

The Scrambler was first marketed in 1955 and came to Bertrand Island in 1961. A double-rotation ride, the Scrambler was located by the park entrance between the Boomerang and the Dodgem.

Off-duty and part-time Mount Arlington police officers continued to handle the park's security needs. The park was fortunate to have experienced few serious police matters over the years.

The June Rose Ballroom evolved into the Bertrand Island Villa and for awhile was dubbed the "Palace" attempting to update its image with rock and roll in the 1970s.

Peter Frampton played Bertrand Island in 1974.

The sites of California Lodge and its Dining Hall became parking areas in the 1940s. The house at the upper left is the old Kraus homestead. Following Louis Kraus's death, it became the home of his daughter and son-in-law, Dorothy and Ed Cuda, who lived there for many years.

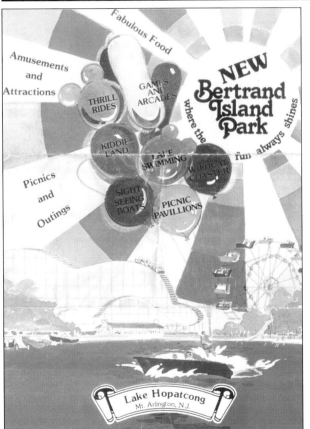

Throughout the 1960s and 1970s, great change was occurring in the amusement park industry. Huge corporate theme parks, beginning with Disneyland and then including such giants as Six Flags and Busch Gardens, were built across America. In the face of such competition, Bertrand Island continued to advertise and compete, even using New York television in its later years.

As larger theme parks gained popularity, many of the older traditional amusement parks found that they could no longer compete. New Jersey's Olympic Park closed in 1965 and Palisades Park succumbed in 1971.

Bertrand Island survived and prospered in the turbulent 1960s and was able to hang on in the 1970s. However, with competition from larger parks and the slowing of the baby boom, the park began to show some wear. Having spent 30 years in charge of the park, Ray D'Agostino became interested in selling.

Larger amusement park operators who toured the park decided that it did not have sufficient land for expansion and, therefore, they were not interested. One of the later attractions at the park was a moon walk added in the 1970s.

Land values around the lake continued to soar, as did real estate taxes and insurance costs. The existence of an "old style" family amusement park at Lake Hopatcong was quickly becoming economically unfeasible. To the left of the Ferris wheel is the Cube, which opened in the 1970s featuring loud music, psychedelic lighting, and lightweight balls patrons could throw at each other.

Ray D'Agostino sold the park in 1978 to Gabriel Warshawsky. Although the new owner continued to operate the park, developing the land was clearly on his mind. Go-carts were a later addition at the park.

Even in its later years, the park continued to add new rides and games. The 1970s saw such additions as bumper boats, the Trabant (seen above), and the Wild Mouse.

Bertrand Island survived long enough to witness the birth of video games. Many teenagers experienced their first game of Pong or Pacman at Bertrand Island's penny arcade. Of course, the penny arcade still offered old favorites from yesteryear as well. The Wild Mouse (seen above) was a small thrill ride during the park's final years.

Disturbed with changes in the way the park was being managed, local residents, once the core of the park's faithful clientele, began to abandon the park. Rumors began to circulate that the park would close. Space Wars Combat (seen above) was another late addition to the park.

Even the successful introduction of a new lakefront Oyster Pub in 1983 could not reverse the inevitable. On Labor Day of 1983, visitors rode the coaster, knocked the hats off, and enjoyed all the other old favorites for the last time.

Bertrand Island experienced one last bit of glory, as Woody Allen filmed scenes for his movie *The Purple Rose of Cairo* on location in the park during the autumn of 1983. Allen's crew brought in rides and signs. Very little footage shot at Bertrand Island made it into the final cut, but one brief sequence filmed in the roller coaster start house is unmistakable for anyone who remembers the park.

Save those tickets . . . for memories that will not fade!